1
A NOTE ABOUT ALLi

The Alliance of Independent Authors

This book is one of a number of self-publishing guidebooks and campaign books for authors produced by the Alliance of Independent Authors (ALLi).

If you haven't yet heard of ALLi, it is a global, non-profit association for self-publishing authors. Our mission is ethics and excellence in self-publishing and we bring together thousands of indie authors all over the world who are united behind this mission.

All our profits are reinvested back into the organization for the benefit of our members—and the wider author community.

ALLi is pronounced "ally" (al-eye), and an ally is what we aim to be to self-publishers everywhere. Our name is spelt with a big ALL and small i because our members are like the three musketeers in Dumas's eponymous novel: ALL working for each individual "i", and each for ALL.

ALLi offers members a range of benefits but our real strength is our members, team and advisors, who provide something like the ancient system of craft apprenticeship, with the wisdom of the hive-mind instead of one master.

Our work is fourfold:
- ALLi *advises*, providing best-practice information and education through a Self-Publishing Advice Center that offers a daily blog, weekly livestreams and podcasts, a bookstore of self-publishing guidebooks, and a quarterly member magazine.
- ALLi *monitors* the self-publishing sector through a **watchdog desk**, alerting authors to bad actors and predatory players and running an approved partner program.
- ALLi *campaigns* for the **advancement of indie authors** in the publishing and literary sectors globally (bookstores, libraries, literary events, prizes, grants, awards, and other author organizations), encouraging the provision of publishing and business skills for authors, speaking out against iniquities, and furthering the indie author cause wherever possible.
- ALLi *empowers* independent authors through a wide variety of **member tools and resources** including author forums, contract advice, sample agreements, networking, literary agency representation, and a member care desk.

Headquartered in London, we operate all over the world and at every level, bringing our mission of ethics and excellence in self-publishing to beginner, emerging and experienced authors. Whether you're just starting out, or you're already widely published, ALLi can empower you to make better books, reach more readers, and generate greater profits.

When you join ALLi, you're not just joining an organization, you're becoming part a transformative, self-organising, global author movement. Whether you're self-publishing your first novel or your fiftieth, ALLi is with you every step of the way, with a suite of member benefits that includes free guidebooks, discounts and deals, member forums, contract consultancy, advisory board, literary agency, watchdog and more.

Your membership also supports our advocacy work for indie authors globally, from Alaska to New Zealand, and offers access to ALLi's supportive, dynamic community.

If you haven't yet, is it time you joined us?

AllianceIndependentAuthors.org

2

INTRODUCTION TO PODCASTING FOR AUTHORS

"Podcasting" is a term that has entered the mainstream only in the last decade. A podcast is a digital audio file that you can download to a computer or mobile device via the internet. It typically takes the form of serial, on-demand episodes and is similar to the format used by radio shows. Listeners subscribe to the podcast, then episodes download automatically to their device through podcast players like iTunes, Stitcher, Spotify and Overcast. If you're reading this, you probably already know what a podcast is and are ready to explore the possibility of podcasting yourself. This guide will show you the way.

Podcasts are mainly speech-based: interviews, talk shows, lectures, panel discussions or quizzes, fiction, drama, poetry, comedy sketches —anything you might hear on speech radio. The unique selling point that distinguishes podcasts from radio shows is the ability to download the audio and listen any time you want. And just like self-publishing versus traditional publishing, podcasting has given rise to a far more diverse and multi-faceted range of content than traditional voice media.

A few years ago, listening to a podcast was a niche interest activity, but as mobile technology evolved, the cultural zeitgeist has shifted.

Thanks to massive demand, access to technology, and the omnipresence of the internet, more people than ever are now recording and listening to podcasts on every possible topic. There are now an estimated two million unique shows, together encompassing 48 million episodes today, according to the Podcast Insights website. Ofcom, the UK's communications regulator, tells us that one in eight people in the UK now listen to at least one podcast episode each week, and the US stats show a similar picture.

Many authors have jumped into the space as listeners, guests, hosts and podcast creators. Learning from peers, authors are using this valuable platform to engage their community and draw attention to their brands and their books.

The idea of hosting, never mind producing a podcast, is daunting for most authors but there's no need to fret. All those author-podcasters who seem so confident have also experienced doubts, imposter syndrome, and overwhelm at times. While podcasting requires skills you are unlikely to have developed yet, concerns diminish with exposure. You will feel some degree of anxiety when approaching such an unfamiliar topic—there's no escaping that—but it's okay to take your time. If you aren't particularly technically savvy, or you experience doubt and anxiety over appearing on a podcast, that's not a reason to forego podcasting.

Ultimately, you will need to figure out whether this medium is right for you and how deeply you want to get involved. This short guidebook will show you how to decide and explain exactly how get started and keep going, in the way that's right for you.

No matter where you're starting from, you can make inroads into podcasting in a way that enables you to build your following, sell more books, and feel more engrained in the lives of your readers and other authors in your niche.

3
HOW TO READ THIS BOOK

This guide is designed to be read chronologically, but we understand that authors' lives are busy, and you may just want to dip into particular sections. So some contextual information has been repeated in multiple chapters. While reading the full guide for context first is advisable, do dive into the chapter you most need most right now, if that's your way of working.

Everyone starts off in the same state of ignorance, but the information outlined within the following pages can be digested and practiced in manageable chunks at whatever speed you deem comfortable. Please note that we cite costs and payments in United States Dollars (USD), unless quoting a source, as it is the most universal currency for indie authors, and many of the dominant service providers are based in the US and operate in USD.

The podcasting industry contains a lot of jargon and this guide contains industry-specific terms and acronyms that you might not have heard of before. These terms can be confusing, even off-putting, at the beginning. While we've given the terms in this book as much context as possible, we've also provided a glossary at the end of the document for easy reference which we hope will prove useful.

Podcasting is an industry in its infancy, and its tools are constantly improving. While this book is up-to-date at the time of writing, some of the tools and processes may have changed by the time you read it.

Read on to learn about the particulars of the industry, what it takes to become a podcaster, and how to be an effective host, guest or producer.

4

THE ASKALLI SELF-PUBLISHING PODCASTS

Before we begin, as you are an indie author, you're likely to be interested in the Alliance of Independent Author (ALLi)'s Self-Publishing Advice Podcast in which the ALLi team dives deep into publishing for authors, at different levels. There is also an interview stream, where members are interviewed about the inspirations behind their books, and a member Q&A in which ALLi member questions are answered.

ADVANCED SELF-PUBLISHING ADVICE PODCAST: ORNA ROSS AND Joanna Penn (video livestream + podcast)

First Friday of the month, you'll get top tips and tools for running a successful author business, plus analysis of the latest self-publishing news and trends. This show is for those who know how to self-publish and want to expand their income and influence. CLICK HERE to tune into ALLi's Advanced Self-Publishing Advice Podcast

MEMBERS' Q&A SELF-PUBLISHING ADVICE PODCAST: ORNA ROSS AND Michael LaRonn (video livestream + podcast)

Second Friday of the month, Orna Ross and Michael LaRonn answer members' most pressing self-publishing questions. All are welcome to listen and learn, but only paid-up ALLi Members can submit questions. CLICK HERE to tune into ALLi Members' Q&A Self-Publishing Advice Podcast. (video livestream + podcast)

Foundational Self-Publishing Advice Podcast: Orna Ross and Dan Parsons

Third Friday of the month, this show explores a theme essential to self-publishers at all levels, particularly those just starting out, from the often differing perspectives of writing fiction or nonfiction. CLICK HERE to learn more about ALLi's Foundational Self-Publishing Advice Salon

Self-Publishing News: Dan Holloway and Howard Lovy (podcast only)

Fourth Friday of the month, Dan Holloway and Howard Lovy discuss the latest news and trends of interest to indie authors. CLICK HERE to tune into ALLi's Self-Publishing News Podcast

Inspirational Indie Author Interview (podcast only)

Every second Sunday, the #AskALLI podcast also offers a weekly **Inspirational Indie Author Interview** in which ALLi's multimedia manager Howard Lovy interviews ALLi members about the inspiration behind their books. CLICK HERE to tune into ALLi's inspirational author Interviews. (If you're an ALLi member who'd like to be interviewed, write to Howard at howard@allianceindependentauthors.org)

5

WHY PODCAST?

Authors have been involved in podcasting from the start, seeing it as an effective way to publicise their books and allow readers to get to know, like and trust them. Since Google Search announced it would be indexing podcast episodes (not just shows), and displaying them on the first page of results alongside video and text, many more authors have developed an interest.

If Google's plans play out as expected, a podcast should prove to be a great discovery tool for authors and books. That doesn't, however, mean it's something every author should do. Yes, if done correctly, podcasting can be a great way to promote your work, but if done poorly, it can take away from your valuable writing time and offer little benefit in return.

Podcasting is an imbalanced industry, just like writing and acting. A minority of shows get the bulk of listeners while most settle in the long tail. You must produce an excellent show and market it well if you want it to succeed and deliver you a readership for your books. Those who do succeed often put in the time and effort to run their podcast like a business. They work hard to make deep connections with their audiences and build a powerful network of guests. Those who don't fully commit usually struggle to build a following.

As with self-publishing, the podcasting gold rush is long over. Releasing a show and instantly getting thousands of listeners without doing any marketing is a thing of the past. It's as difficult to market a podcast as a book—so why bother? And a lot of work and financial investment is required to make a successful podcast. So, is it worth it?

These are good questions, and the answers depend on your goals. If you're passionate about this area and want to make podcasting a key part of your business, then taking the time to build your own listenership is absolutely worth it. A podcast appears regularly and so gives more regular marketing opportunities than a book. In comparison to the fragmented connection established by social media, a podcast allows you to engage your audience on your own website, with your voice. Many readers find podcasts more convenient to consume than blog posts. They can listen while driving, walking, working out, or doing chores around the house. Hence, by running a show, you can potentially reach a lot of listeners who wouldn't otherwise engage with you. Add the fact that there are at least 600 million blogs and 23 million YouTube channels, but only 800,000 podcasts in Apple Podcasts, and you will realize that hosting a podcast gives you a competitive edge in a relatively uncrowded market. As few authors manage to sustain a regular podcast, managing one successfully can be a real way to stand out to individual listeners.

Owning your own podcast IP can also deliver ancillary opportunities. You can get a transcript of the podcast and then repurpose it into blog posts, social media, and ad content. People say "yes" more often to podcast interviews than to blog interviews where they have to write answers to questions, so an interview show gives you a better opportunity to make personal connections with other authors and experts in your niche. And many of these connections will help you with your own book launches. They will join your tribe.

There is a reason why only a minority of podcasts do well, though. Despite the many advantages a successful podcast host enjoys, podcasting must be integrated with your existing writing and publishing framework for it to work. If you're not passionate about the thoughts of running a show on your chosen topic, it's best not to waste all the time it takes to set up and run a show, only for it to fizzle out after a few months.

Deciding not to produce your own show is not deciding that you shouldn't get involved in podcasting at all. You can always pitch existing podcasters to be a guest on their show. You won't get all of the benefits that a host gets, but you won't have to wrestle with all of their headaches either.

Cultural Adoption

More people are listening to podcasts than ever before. According to Edison Research, the number of Americans listening to a podcast each week has grown 120% over the past four years, and 90 million Americans listen to a podcast every month. It's a similar story in Canada, where 36% of people now listen to podcasts monthly, up from 28% the previous year. The same goes for the rest of the English-speaking world. Over 1.6 million Australians now download audio or video podcasts in an average four-week window, up from under 1 million just four years ago.

The most popular podcasting device still is the Apple iPhone—it was the first to make serious ground with podcasts and has a built-in app—though there are listening options for every mobile, tablet device, and computer. Indeed, most podcast directories now cater for users on both Apple and Android devices and accept content from creators of all backgrounds. This universal access is expected to grow now that Spotify more widely accepts podcasts and other tech giants are weighing in on the space.

Judging by the data, the trend will continue, and more people than ever will soon adopt listening to podcasts as one of their favorite pastimes. Inevitably, money will follow, and more prominent hosts and guests will grow to become household names. Hence, now is a great time to get involved because we're at a phase in which there is growing demand and still relatively low competition (when compared to other platforms like blogging and vlogging). Put simply, now is a great time to join the podcasting movement.

Innovations in Cars

There has been a steady increase in the number of people listening to podcasts on the go. The reason for this is simple: many smartphone owners now have a constant connection to the internet and enough data allowance to consume anything on a near-constant basis. They take full advantage of this freedom, listening hands-free to content everywhere from the grocery store to the daily commute, whether by bus, train, or car.

According to a 2019 study by Edison Media/Triton Digital, 26% of adults in the United States listen to a podcast while driving. That rate has increased 1% from the previous year and 7% from 2017. This is something to keep in mind when recording a podcast. The rumble of the engine on the road will play into the experience for an increasing number of listeners, so ensuring a high-quality audio is of paramount importance.

Yes, this car listenership complicates matters for creators, but it also shows the scale and growth potential for podcasts in general. As the technology becomes more integrated into automobiles, the percentage of people who use cars to consume content will only go one way—up. It's already easy to listen with Apple CarPlay, which is considered a safe way to access iPhone apps in a car.

Many recent car models have this capability or a similar solution as a standard feature now. They simplify hands-free listening. All a listener has to do before embarking on a trip (if they don't have enough mobile data to access the internet at all times) is download a podcast then connect their phone to their car using a USB port or wireless Bluetooth technology. After that, everything appears on the car's screen. If data usage isn't a problem though, they don't even need to go to the trouble of pre-downloading. They can stream live to the car.

This functionality is generations ahead of the humble CD, but it's about to make yet another quantum leap if self-driving cars hit the mainstream. When people need to concentrate less while driving at all, more of them will no doubt consume content while they travel.

Innovations in Homes

By now, many of us are intimately familiar with the phrases "Hey, Alexa!" and "Okay, Google!," so much so that the AIs that power them could be considered members of our family. This is because voice-recognition technology has advanced massively in recent years and, as a result, voice assistants have become commonplace in the modern world. They don't just provide a hands-free search alternative on smartphones and tablets, but are also integrated into our homes.

As such, they have made listening to content far easier than in the past. Without even having to stand, anyone can request a podcast or music and have it follow them around the house, hopping the feed from one speaker to another. All the while, their owners can get on with whatever it is they want to do, never needing to be near the device, which has furthered the adoption rates of podcasts and is likely to continue to do so in the future.

Key Takeaways

In summary, you should consider podcasting because:

- Technological advancements and cultural shifts have caused them to grow in popularity
- Commuters can now listen easily hands-free in their cars
- Voice assistant innovations mean that more people than ever are listening in their homes

6

TYPES OF PODCASTS FOR AUTHORS

There are a variety of podcast formats that you can follow as a host, all of which can work well. As with every aspect of the publishing business though, there is no perfect format that works for everyone. There are many variables to factor into your decision-making process when creating a podcast. Much depends on your genre and niche, audience expectations, and your goals. For example, you might want a podcast that has a narrative element designed to target fantasy readers, or you might want a business podcast full of interviews you can use to expand your personal network and knowledge.

In each case, think about what will appeal to your readers or target audience. What can you uniquely offer them? What idea feels like fun to you? You are more likely to stick with your venture and be successful if you cover all three elements. Below are a few examples of the various podcast styles you may want to consider that can work for authors.

Interviews

These podcasts feature a single host who interviews individuals within a particular industry. Their draw is the knowledge and insights they provide for their listeners. Examples include:

- The Creative Penn
- The Self-Publishing Show
- The Tim Ferriss Show

Scripted Nonfiction

These are serial podcasts that sometimes have a single theme for a full season, but can also be educational and zero in on a different aspect of a topic on each episode. Examples include:

- Serial
- The 7-Figure Principles Podcast
- Hardcore History

News

Hosts following this format usually summarize the news within a specific industry like publishing, sports, or politics. Examples include:

- The Sell More Books Show
- Bloomberg Surveillance
- Accidental Tech Podcast

Comedy

This podcast type aims to be funny above all else. There are instances of fiction and nonfiction ones. They can have a single host, but many have multiple hosts or guests who bounce off one another. They typically follow a panel show format or provide a commentary on content. Examples include:

- My Dad Wrote a Porno
- No Such Thing As Fish
- Fake Doctors, Real Friends with Zach and Donald

Poetry Analysis

Poetry podcasters tend to delve into the meaning, craft, or celebration of poetry by analyzing a different poem or talking to a different guest poet each episode. Examples include:

- Poem Talk
- Frank Skinner's Poetry Podcast
- The Poetry Society

Scripted Fiction

These podcasts are similar to scripted radio dramas and are often highly produced. Hosts act out fiction, much like an audiobook narrator, and include an array of sound effects. Examples include:

- The Magnus Archives
- Limetown
- CARAVAN

Key Takeaways

When coming up with a format for a podcast, you should consider the genre you write, your personal goals, audience expectations, and the function you want your podcast to serve *before* selecting from the following options:

- Interviews
- Scripted nonfiction
- News
- Comedy
- Poetry analysis
- Scripted fiction

7

GETTING STARTED

There is no one path that all indie authors must follow to be successful. From publishing, to distribution, to marketing, each stage can be executed in a hundred different ways. And, though you might be tempted to try them all, that will only stretch your attention too thinly to be effective at any one strategy. The same goes for podcasting.

Podcasting authors commonly face tons of choices and experience a constant sense of overwhelm. If you're new to the industry, you've probably sampled a variety of podcast types and know some marketing strategies, but don't really know which of them will work for you. Begin on your own and you risk acting like a dog chasing cars, lacking direction, and never getting what you want. Luckily, there is a way to filter out a lot of the noise and find a strategy that will work for you, which we will explore in this chapter. It's simple: follow your readers.

From branding to your show format to marketing strategies, your readers should inform every decision you make. You might think that's restrictive. On the contrary, knowing your readers' preferences can help you to filter out time-wasting busywork and narrow your focus so that every action you make pushes you closer to achieving your objective. All it takes is a bit of research and forethought.

Here are the steps that give a podcast a good chance of success.

Find Your Audience

Once you've worked out what type of show you want to create, then you need to determine if that type has an existing audience and find out where those people currently hang out. Doing so will inform your creative decisions and help to shape your marketing activities so that they are more effective.

The easiest place to begin your research is online. When starting a new podcast, simply pop open Apple Podcasts, Stitcher, or Spotify and see if there are any similar podcasts to the one you want to create that are successful. If there are, that means there's a market for it. If there aren't, you need to dig a little deeper. A lack of any similar presence could mean there isn't an audience for that market or that you've stumbled upon an underserved niche.

After you've found similar shows, listen to them to figure out the most popular show formats and where the hosts reach their listeners. For instance, they might mention hosting private communities on their own websites or a particular social media platform. This is a good way to learn who your potential audience is instead of trying to guess. Knowing where they are allows you to join their community and become an active member to determine their likes and dislikes as well as to build relationships.

Even if no individual site it mentioned when you listen to the market-leading podcasts, you can usually make an educated guess when you listen to the topics of conversation on each show. If the host mentions school or talks about young adult books, then you might want to look into establishing a presence on a social media platform with a statistically younger user demographic, such as TikTok or YouTube. If they talk about military history, then Facebook might be the best place to spend your time because it's full of millennials, generation X, and baby boomers who tend to favor that genre.

• • •

ProTip: Don't aim to promote yourself when joining these online communities. Instead, provide value to the community so that they learn to know, like, and trust you, and then see you as an authority on your chosen subject. Your contributions will do much of the promotion for you.

Collect Episode Ideas

Every audience is different. Spend some time talking to your ideal listeners and you will discover that they have individual wants and needs. Though some will be unique, others will come up often. Begin an idea list of episode topics based on popular subjects they discuss or pain points that you think you could soothe. Some you'll use, and some you won't. There are no rules at this stage, just ideas.

One thing to consider is how much free time your audience has at their disposal. Those who live busy lifestyles, like entrepreneurs, might not have a lot of time and crave bite-sized pieces of information delivered frequently. If you're catering to them, then short, snappy podcast episodes packed with actionable content might be best. Painters, on the other hand, might prefer long-form content that they can digest slowly over an hour or two while creating art.

Ask yourself, "How do my ideal listeners live and think?" If you're uncertain, keep researching successful podcasts. Don't plagiarize their ideas, but it's fine to take inspiration from multiple sources and creating something new.

Key Takeaways

In summary, to start developing a podcast idea, you should:

- Figure out your reasons and goals
- Find out where your ideal audience exists and join the community
- Collect episode ideas based on talking points

8

DESIGNING YOUR SHOW

Author podcasts are as varied as the authors that create them. Each one has a different hosting style, format order, audience demographic, and creator objective. The form is still evolving, so innovation is rife at all stages of the creative process, from naming conventions to artwork to merchandising. How you design and present your show is up to you. The only limit to what you can do with a podcast is your own imagination.

That said, there are established practices that will give your ideas a better chance of thriving. For instance, it helps to consider some of the following fundamental questions before you settle on a name and commission logo artwork:

- Why are you starting a podcast?
- What will be the tone and subject matter of your show?

If you aren't sure how to answer these questions, sometimes f-r-e-e-writing can help. The concept is simple: sit down with a pen and paper, and write a stream of consciousness (fast, raw, exact-and-easy) answering the questions asked. This provides clarity and brings subconscious and semi-conscious thoughts and desires to the forefront, to guide your actions.

Once you've answered the whys and whats, identify your podcasting goals. To phrase it another way, what's the purpose of your podcast, and what outcome do you want it to deliver?

Here are some common goals in podcasting to give you ideas:

- To generate book sales
- To be recognized as an expert in your niche
- To share an important message
- To connect with a particular group of readers

It's helpful to write your answers down so you can refer back to them as you develop your show's concept. You may have more than one goal. If you do, note them all. You're looking for a podcast concept that unifies them. Coming up with a strong vision at an early stage will stop you from having to pivot after you've already built an established brand.

Choose a Theme

When you've settled on the audience you want to target and the goals you want to achieve, it's time to move from a general concept to a specific theme. This will be your niche—an idea around which you will orbit to build your defined audience over time. Examples include:

- Producing scripted LitRPG
- Teaching how to become a digital nomad
- The mindset of professional athletes

Your theme can be broad or narrow, but you must be passionate about whatever you choose. It should be something you're excited to research and discuss on a regular basis. Sticking to your theme is what will keep your core audience engaged with your content.

Once you have an idea of what to podcast about, do market research. Search your show's topic on Spotify or Apple Podcasts. Listen to episodes of similar shows to see what they do well and think of ways they could improve. When you get an idea for a theme, look at the podcast charts to see if there are any shows already covering the cornerstone topics you have in mind. Are there many similar podcasts? If there are, then that's not necessarily a bad thing. The fact that they're in the chart just proves that there is demand for the type of content you want to create. What's different about your show is what could help it stand out from the rest.

If you still can't tell whether there is an existing demand for your ideas after that activity, do some keyword analysis. This sounds complicated, but it basically means finding out what people are searching. It's easy when you know how. For example, let's say you're looking to create a podcast that talks about popular TV shows. You could type the names of those shows into Google Trends and compare their search traffic, looking for TV shows that get searched a lot but aren't being covered by other podcasts. Alternatively, you could visit Answer the Public and type in your topic. In response, the site presents a list of popularly searched questions that relate to it.

Ideally you want to find ideas that are:

- Popular enough to attract organic traffic
- Not so competitive that your podcast gets buried by competitors

This research will inform your theme. It's okay to pick one that's already popular as long as you believe that your unique take will be enough to grab attention. Just be sure that your theme has enough longevity to stay interesting for you and to generate enough long-term content that offer a steady stream of ideas. What notes are you already curating or collecting? What do people ask you about all the time? On what subjects do you have special insights or expertise? All of these questions can help you pick an effective theme.

Beware, though, if you are a multi-genre writer. Like readers, podcast listeners can be choosy. Many have strong genre and topical preferences. If you try to cover too many ideas, you'll alienate potential listeners. As a result, the best strategy is to find a theme that will encapsulate your identity and appeal to as many listeners as possible without diluting your brand.

If some of your ideas don't have an overlapping audience at all, then it's wise to choose. Pick one, and podcast only about that if you want to capture a defined audience. That's a proven way to form a cohesive brand and gather superfans. If you really want to appeal to two distinct audiences, then you could mash them together in one podcast and risk losing the interest of many, or you could create a second show once you've gained more experience.

Pin Down a Format

We've already defined the main podcast formats in a previous chapter, but they're worth re-mentioning because your format provides a framework for your theme and overall brand. Some podcasts just have a single host, others are scripted stories, others are in-depth interviews. The key question you need to contemplate is whether you are going to podcast your work with readings, drama, or performance, or whether you are going to podcast *about* your work with interviews or a commentary.

You must choose one format that fits your podcast theme but, even more importantly, your personality and preferences. If you love improvisation and witty banter, you will need guests and maybe a co-host. If you like having everything scripted, what about an audio drama or poetry reading?

Develop a Name

It's worth taking time to come up with a few podcast name ideas rather than settling on the first one that pops into your head. A podcast with a good name can drastically outperform a competitor that isn't named effectively. When choosing yours, try to pick something catchy, memorable, and easy to spell. That will make it easier to search and will aid word-of-mouth virality. Using simple words is best because they align with what the average person will search.

Keywords must play a part in your decision-making process. Not only can they generate more organic traffic on podcast platforms, but well-selected keywords can also help to promote the nuances of your podcast to attract its ideal listeners. Ideally, you'll want to include relevant keywords that deliver high traffic but low competition.

Avoid keyword stuffing, however—stuffing your metadata with a repeated keyword to the point of not sounding human simply to rank more highly in search results. You want to make it easy for people to find your podcast, but not come across as someone who's gaming the system. Simplicity is the best approach to achieve a balance. If you have a short podcast name, add a brief description in the title tag to help search results.

Here are some examples:

• *Akimbo*: **A Podcast from Seth Godin**. Most people searching for this podcast search for Seth Godin himself because he has a strong following. So, his name is included in the title.

• **The** *Self-Publishing Advice Podcast* **from the Alliance of Independent Authors**. On this ALLi podcast, we give advice for indie authors, so we use the keyword "self-publishing advice" to rank well on that topic.

• *Tasty Web Development Treats from Syntax*. There probably aren't many people searching for "Syntax" unless they already know the show. As a result, including "web development" in the podcast name significantly increases the odds of being discovered by those who are interested in web development.

The best way for you to choose your name depends on your situation. Is your favorite name idea catchy and easy to spell? Are you famous? Have you included relevant keywords? Strike the right balance and your podcast name can pay dividends down the line.

Create Artwork

Commissioning artwork can be expensive. If you can't design your own podcast logo and branding images, then the costs can range from $50 to over $1,000. For this reason, unless you're already an experienced podcaster it's wise to hold off on creating artwork until you've produced a few episodes and have worked out the look and feel of your show. Your concept is likely to evolve as you record more shows and gain feedback from your early listeners over social media. Running jokes will emerge, slogans will materialize, and your interviews or segments will take a detour as you follow your creative muse and find your voice as a host. Your early experiences may lead you to change your topic, title, or even theme. Start with a placeholder graphic if you're new to all of this and you can update when ready with something more professional.

Key Takeaways

In summary, when designing your podcast, you should:

- Choose a theme that is popular and will enthuse you for a long time
- Identify the best format for your personality
- Develop a name that is catchy, easy to spell, and good for SEO
- Wait until you've recorded a few episodes before paying for artwork

9

FOLLOWING A PRODUCTION PROCESS

As a prospective podcast creator, you're probably full of enthusiasm and ready to start creating. Fortunately you can, once you've finished your market research. What you'll soon discover, though, is that podcasting is harder than it looks. While creating your first few episodes, you'll probably run into problems. That's normal. You'll also take longer than you thought you would, and the result won't be half as polished as you would like it to be. That's also normal.

At the beginning, starting is all that matters. You need to produce work in order to see your flaws and improve—the more work the better! As successful YouTuber and podcaster Ali Abdaal puts it, "I found that by focusing on quantity, it developed the habit of video editing [...] and the quality naturally came out of that." Hence, the logic here is simple: get the low-quality early attempts out of your system, and use them as a learning opportunity. Knowing where to start can be a challenge without prior experience, but there's no need to worry because we've created a production process to guide your early creations.

Set a SMART Goal

The best way to get started is to figure out what you want, set a clear goal to keep yourself on track, and achieve it. This goal should be:

- Specific
- Measurable
- Achievable
- Realistic
- Time-bound

WRITE IT DOWN TO REMIND YOURSELF OF YOUR GOAL SO THAT YOU DON'T go off track. An example would read like this:

> "I want to create a podcast for thriller authors and release one episode a week for the rest of the year, resulting in 25 episodes by New Year's Eve."

HAVING A SMART GOAL ENABLES YOU TO ESTABLISH WHAT YOU WANT IN a specific, measurable way that is achievable. It's best to focus on getting process-based results, rather than results that rely on other people, because it gives you more control and makes you less likely to get demotivated by uncontrollable factors. That's why releasing "one episode a week" is a better goal than "get 1,000 new listeners a week." It's something you can achieve because you don't have to rely on other people to make it happen.

Step One: Outline

Hit record without an episode plan and you'll discover that talking smoothly on cue isn't easy. Unless you know the topic you want to discuss, you'll waffle and quickly lose the interest of your early listeners. Recording doesn't work like writing, where you can feel your way into the dark, because podcast words can't be edited in quite the same way. In many respects, your first draft can be cleaned up, but a podcast is basically your final draft, so planning and rehearsal is necessary.

At the very least to make a good show, you need to develop an outline. When creating your first episode, look at the list of topics you brainstormed. (You did that, right?) Choose one that excites you. Then make a bulleted outline of the points you plan to discuss. Make sure each one is tight and relevant and allows for a smooth transition from point to point. If you plan to interview a guest, share your planned questions with them. You don't need to be too detailed. In most cases, a few short bullet points are enough to keep you on track.

Step Two: Write Beats

The writing world is divided into plotters and pantsers: those who plot out their books in minute detail before writing their first drafts and those who write by the seat of their pants, discovering the story as they type. Which category you fall into will likely shape how you carry out the next stage of your podcast.

Most podcasters outline to some degree. You have a few options beyond the initial bullet points. You can either hit record and riff on the notes you've already written, or you can grow your outline into a series of beats—or sub-points—then script entire episodes before getting in front of the mic. If you think you don't need more planning or that your chosen format works best without it, you should choose the former option. But if you value control and perfectionism, then the latter might be better for you.

Either way, unless you're experienced and comfortable behind a mic or gifted with the ability to speak extemporaneously, scripting the parts of your first episode that you need to get right, like your intro or sponsor slots, is usually a good idea at a minimum. It'll help you wrap your head around the structure of the podcast and get you comfortable with recording yourself. The key is to experiment to see what ends up feeling the most comfortable for you and what style resonates with your chosen audience.

Step Three: Practice

Doing anything new is uncomfortable at first. You might hate reaching out to guests and feel anxiety a moment before you begin recording. You might hit your mic and cough when your throat goes dry. You might also hate listening to your voice the first few times you sit down to edit the result. That's totally normal.

Be that as it may, everyone experiences a similar learning curve. Just because you didn't have a good initial experience, that doesn't mean future attempts will be just as scary or awkward. Try to be as objective as you can when reviewing what you've produced, and remember that you aren't there to judge yourself—you're there to judge the quality of the product. Don't aim to be better than a podcasting A-lister; aim to be better than your last episode.

Ask yourself:

- How long is the podcast, and do you need to work on pacing?
- Do you sound meek or like you're reading a news report?
- Do you get gabby and veer off topic?
- How can you improve?

ANSWER THESE QUESTIONS, AND RECORD AGAIN IF YOU RECORDED ALONE and didn't hit the mark. If you have guests that can't return for a second recording, edit your episodes as best you can and move on, vowing to be better in the future. The key is to view your early episodes as on-the-job training. Practice and keep going until it becomes second nature. Perseverance is the difference between those who become accomplished broadcasters and those who give up before they see success.

Key Takeaways

In summary, when producing an episode, you should:

- Write a SMART goal for podcast production
- Jot down your talking points to have an idea of what to say
- Create a series of beats or possibly a script, depending on your format and experience level
- Practice and allow yourself to improve by creating imperfect early episodes

10

USING EQUIPMENT

There is a range of equipment you need to record a podcast. Some podcasters have professional set-ups, but it doesn't need to be that way. For every $1,000 device, there is a $50 alternative or sometimes free software that can do a similar job. It's worth spending some money on equipment, but you don't need to fork out a fortune to create an above-average show.

Consider the production level you want to achieve and whether you are going to be doing a solo show or one with co-hosts and/or guests. Also, will those co-hosts and guests be remote or in the same location as you? All these factors dictate the kind of equipment you need. In this section, we will break down common items that podcasters use to record and produce their shows, factoring in a variety of budgets so that you can weigh the costs and benefits yourself.

A Room

This isn't technically equipment, but it's relevant. You need space to record a podcast—usually enough to hold a table, computer, and a recording mic. You can have a set-up that features multiple chairs for hosts and live guests, but there's no need to go that far if you don't have the room. These days, thanks to Zoom, Skype, and other similar companies, you don't need room for guests, and many won't travel anyway.

It's often actually easier to have guests and co-hosts based at separate locations, connected via communication software, than it is to try and record multiple people in the same location. That way, you don't have to worry about setting up multiple mics and the interference that happens when they're close to one another.

A Computer

You will need access to a desktop computer or laptop. A PC or Apple Mac will do. Most computers have more than enough processing power to handle audio files, so there's no need to get a top-of-the-range model unless you're in a position to afford one.

Communication Software

Skype and Zoom have been the leading video-conference software options for podcasters for some time. As a result of their ample functionality and the fact that many guests are intimately familiar with how they work, you can't go wrong sticking with these brands. Both can be downloaded for free but have paid alternatives if you want the extra functionality that they keep behind a paywall.

Microphone Paraphernalia

If there is only one person being recorded locally, you can create a decent show by purchasing a relatively inexpensive USB microphone. The ATR2100 microphone is popular among new podcasters, simply because it is both a USB and an XLR microphone and is relatively inexpensive (about $65 when not on sale). Outside the US, where the ATR2100 is more expensive, the Samson Q2U microphone is considered a similar but more affordable alternative. The XLR connector option allows you to use the same microphone if you later choose to move to a more advanced set-up.

The Blue Yeti is a more expensive but popular USB-only microphone that many podcasters use successfully. It's robust, easy to use, and comes with a multitude of recording mode options. It's a good investment if you don't plan to upgrade anytime soon after making an initial mic purchase. If you do use a Blue Yeti as a podcast host, make sure to set it to "Cardioid Mode" where it takes the sound from directly in front of the microphone rather than the whole room. That can provide you with a crisper sound and less background noise. Throw a pop filter and a mic stand into the set-up and you will drastically reduce interference from plosive mouth sounds and desk vibrations.

Recording Software

You need to use a program to record either your voice or a Skype call. For solo shows, Audacity works well. Or, if you plan to run an interview-based podcast, you can record Skype calls using programs such as Pamela (which is PC-based) or ECamm Call Recorder (which is Mac-based).

There are also specialist services like Cleanfeed which are designed to record both sides of the call and replace Skype. These software programs can deliver better results in some situations, but require your guest or co-host to install a browser plug-in to make that happen. Sometimes this can cause unintended inconvenience.

If you want to add extra flexibility for guests, you could use Skype Credits to call standard telephone numbers from the program. Connecting to someone's phone via your Skype account can help you to nab superstar guests if that's the only way they'll communicate, but this option can sometimes lead to inferior sound quality. Alternatively, you could connect yourself and your guest to Audacity (which is called doing a "double-ender") and then take both tracks and combine them in post-production. All of these options are possible, but whether you should use them will depend on your technical ability and how accommodating you want to be for guests.

Recording Hardware

A final option is to use a more traditional audio equipment set-up, including professional hardware. The initial set-up cost is more expensive, and using a range of gear can be complicated. Then, after all that, the extra effort and expense only results in an increase of about 10% to15% in audio quality. However, if you have the expertise and funds to make this possible, it might be an option you want to explore, especially if you want to make your podcast an enhanced auditory experience.

Using specialist equipment does have some advantages:

- You can use higher quality microphones (with XLR connections).
- Having a separate digital recorder means you won't lose a whole episode if your computer crashes, and you'll need to record only from the point that you lost connection.
- Setting up a mixer with volume levels and EQ settings can reduce your post-production workload.
- You need to run less software on your PC, which leads to fewer crashes.
- If you want to record multiple people in one location, then a mixer lets you connect them to one device.
- If you have an external sound card, then you can mute all your PC's system sounds and send Skype out to an external sound card.

Before attempting this kind of set-up, it's wise to read a few tutorials and articles on the subject to get solid advice that will save you time and money. An advanced set-up might be tempting, but always remember that technology follows the law of diminishing returns. If you're a beginner, it's best to stick with the basics. Upgrade your system slowly once you're sure that podcasting is right for you and you're more comfortable with the equipment you already own.

Key Takeaways

In summary, the equipment you will need to record podcasts include:

- Enough room for you, some equipment, and possibly guests
- A computer with enough processing power to handle audio files
- Communication software like Zoom or Skype
- A decent microphone
- Recording software
- Recording hardware if you want a professional set-up

11

ENSURING HIGH-QUALITY AUDIO

Podcasting is a competitive arena. At one point in history, it was the realm of amateurs. Now, as adoption rates have exploded, more professionals than ever are moving into the space. Those that have been there a while have upped their game considerably. As a result, average podcast listeners now expect crisp sound when listening through headphones and speakers.

As a host, you are the listeners' companion while they commute, do chores, exercise, and relax in their homes. They spend countless hours listening to you. Hence, they have high standards, and so should you. Annoying extra sounds, mumbled dialogue, and other flaws can cause listeners to turn off a show or unsubscribe. This might seem harsh if the content is good, but that's the reality of working as a podcaster.

Thankfully, there is much that can be done to help you avoid this fate, from using the right equipment, to setting your gear to appropriate modes, to cleaning up your product with editing. Establishing good recording habits can be challenging, particularly if you're new and don't have a nuanced ear, but it's worth it. In this chapter, you will learn some basic tips on how to improve your audio quality to make your podcast the best it can be.

Record Locally

If you have a guest on your show, then the best way to ensure that all parties have high-quality audio is to invite them to your studio and record the clean audio yourself. If that isn't possible (not everyone has the luxury of a studio), you can still have a remote conversation using Skype, Zoom, or another similar service. In that case, best practices indicate that both parties should record their side of the conversation on their own local computer using a high-quality microphone.

There are many choices of software that can cater for local recordings. The easiest to use include Quicktime (Mac only) or Audacity (for Mac and PC). If you don't mind paying, many professionals use Adobe Audition. Whichever you use, ensure the recording software is set to pick up sound from your USB microphone and does not automatically adjust your microphone settings.

If you're using Skype or Zoom while recording, setting your preferences is important. Be sure to test all of the recording levels beforehand, and aim for moderate settings that pick up everything you say but don't create an artificial sound that is too muffled, sensitive, or tinny. Do all of this right, and the end result—after editing the two locally recorded halves of the conversation together—will sound as though you and your guests are both in the same room. This will improve the "intimate conversation" experience.

Optimize Your Mic Set-Up

A good USB microphone is essential. The Blue Yeti is a popular and effective option which, for about a hundred bucks, does a fantastic job. There are other options out there if you're working on a smaller budget and most are a step above the built-in microphone on your computer.

Many podcasters stop there but, for best results, you should also include a pop filter. This filter reduces plosive sounds that happen when you pronounce Ps, Bs, and Ts as well as blowing sounds that come from Ss and Ws. Using a good pop filter allows you to place your mouth close to the microphone for a crisp sound without air puffs that tarnish the recording quality. Another option is to include a microphone stand to prevent your computer fan or your hands from interfering with the recording quality.

Podcast hosts often plug in their microphones but forget to change their computer settings. A mistake like this forces them to waste time re-recording their content when they realize they've recorded a whole episode using the wrong mic. So, each time you're about to record, plug in your USB microphone and ensure your audio set-up is connected to it. Your aim should be to enable your USB device rather than the internal microphone.

If you have a bidirectional microphone, make sure it's set for unidirectional recording and faces your mouth. Bidirectional works best if you have a guest in the same studio with you, but it only hampers your recording quality if you're recording alone or interviewing a guest online.

Also, make sure you use headphones or earbuds either plugged into your computer or connected via Bluetooth. Do not use your computer speakers to listen to your co-host. If you do, your mic will pick up their voice on your end, spoiling the pristine recording of your half of the conversation.

When you're sure you have everything in place, hit the "record" button on your local recorder a few seconds before the show starts. You will likely make a few mistakes regarding your set-up when you begin, but this will become a natural routine as you gain experience.

Remove Ambient Noise

Your bodily functions generate more noise than you might release. You probably aren't aware of anything less significant than a loud tummy rumble, but good microphones pick up on a lot more than the human ear. Podcasters often discover tongue clicks, throat groans, and instances of passing air after they're done recording and have difficulty editing these out before hitting publish. As a result, it's wise to prepare your body before sitting down to record a podcast episode.

First ... hydrate! Have a glass of water with you. One thing that listeners don't like to hear is mouth noises, like gurgles and clicks. Taking a drink while your guest is speaking helps prevent these and doesn't break conversation flow. In fact, consider your body in general. For instance, digestion is probably a bigger issue than you might think. Expert audiobook narrator Lorelei King gives good advice on this topic on *The Creative Penn Podcast* when she says:

"Hydration, of course. [...] And eat. You have to keep up your blood sugar. That's why in studios they have a lot of bananas. Bananas are great because they're not very noisy as you digest them."
    Lorelei King

That's a good point about the blood sugar, too. Ensuring you're well-rested works in your favor because it will translate into a happy-sounding host. Believe it or not, podcasting is incredibly draining unless you're a professional who's used to it. Even with this due diligence, you will still need to edit out unwanted ambient noises like digestion and lip smacking. It just helps if they are minimized in the first place.

Phones and computer notifications are another story. They can be omitted entirely if you plan in advance. Create as much of a sound-free environment as possible. If you can't eradicate unwanted noises altogether, then make an effort to get as close as possible. Recording in a small room with good padding helps because it reduces echoes. Also, try to keep children and pets occupied while recording. Wear headphones, too, but don't let the chords hit your clothing as you speak. And beware the buzz of refrigerators.

There's a lot to consider, but reducing ambient noise can massively improve audio quality, save you time in the editing stage, and keep your listeners happy.

Minimize Background Hiss

You've probably heard audio that comes with a background hiss. This hiss is a noise floor—the sum of all background noise signals other than the main one that is being recorded. It usually appears more prominently in amateur audio recordings because the creators record in spaces that aren't designed for recording high-quality audio. You will always get some form of noise floor when recording a podcast, but it is possible to reduce the hiss if you follow a series of quality-improving actions.

Checking your mic sensitivity, positioning, and levels is an important first step. If your mic is set too quietly, you must increase the volume of the whole recording in the editing phase, creating the familiar background hiss. Experiment with microphone positioning and your level settings to reach the optimum set-up for your situation.

If you see wavy lines in the waveform when checking your level settings on-screen, there's too much hiss. If your mic has been used correctly, you will see a near-straight line when sitting silently in front of your mic. Just ensure you don't straighten out the waveform too much using artificial methods because that can cause your voice to sound tinny.

Cutting out background hiss is important when you stitch two tracks together. Having too much hiss on one side of the conversation can make the editing more obvious and cause one speaker to drown out the other. It is best to mute one track while the opposite person is speaking. This can all be done in the editing phase. Stitching and muting two sides of a conversation in this way will make your screen look a bit like a jigsaw puzzle, but the result will be clear sound that is uninterrupted by extraneous noise, which your listeners will appreciate.

None of the physical or technical preparation and the sound-editing tricks outlined in this chapter require years of specialized training or expensive equipment. They can be executed on a home computer and perfected with just a little bit of practice. Yet, these simple techniques will help give your podcast the professional-quality sound it needs to compete in the competitive market.

Key Takeaways

In summary, to ensure high-quality audio, you should:

- Record yourself separately from your guests, who should also record locally
- Optimize your mic's physical set-up and digital settings
- Hydrate, eat a banana, and remove pets or children to reduce ambient noise
- Endeavor to reduce background hiss as much as possible

12

HOSTING

You should record your podcast audio to the highest standard you can manage. For most people, this means saving a wav file. However, wav filetypes aren't supported by many podcast apps, so you'll need to convert your files to mp3 or m4a files before you can submit them for hosting.

While in theory it's possible to store mp3 files on a normal WordPress site, average website hosting is not designed to support the bandwidth of 30-minute audio shows so you'll typically need to pay for specialist media hosting for your podcast. After you've made your first podcast episode, you need to create an RSS feed to make it available on the various podcast networks. RSS stands for RDF Site Summary, or Really Simple Syndication, depending on who you talk to, and is a record-like filetype that collects web content from internet-based outlets.

All you need to know is that it gets updated each time you create a new episode and tells applications, such as Apple Podcasts or Spotify, that a new episode is available, where it is located, and information like the description, episode number, and whether the show is explicit.

. . .

THE RSS FEED IS TYPICALLY CREATED ONE OF THREE WAYS:

- By a plug-in on a WordPress site, for example, Blubrry's PowerPress plug-in
- By a media host like Libsyn
- Create and update manually on a web server by a tech-savvy podcast host

If your podcast only has a niche listenership, and so is unlikely to receive many downloads, then using the PowerPress plug-in and hosting your audio files on a web-based service like Amazon S3 is a good option for you. This is because Amazon S3 charges for the bandwidth a podcast uses, not a set subscription, which can work out better if you only get a small number of downloads. This option is, however, a lot more difficult to set up than just using a company like Libsyn.

So, besides creating an RSS file manually, how do you decide on which media host to choose and where to host your RSS file? Even though the hosting company Blubrry provides the PowerPress plug-in, it doesn't mean that you need to use this in conjunction with Blubrry's hosting. Similarly, Blubrry will provide you with a free WordPress instance if you don't want to host your podcast on your own WordPress website.

The advantages of hosting your RSS Feed on a WordPress site include:

- Being able to save money hosting multiple podcasts on one hosting plan, unlike Libsyn where you have to pay per podcast.
- Being able to upload your mp3 files to a new host without losing your RSS feed if your original hosting company goes bankrupt.
- Having access to cheaper cloud-based storage options for your mp3 files, like Amazon S3.

Meanwhile, the disadvantages of hosting your RSS Feed on a WordPress site include the:

- Extra work required to set up the PowerPress plug-in.
- Strain on your WordPress server that the necessary plug-in causes.
- Fact that your podcast goes down if your WordPress site is down.
- Added complexity of managing your own RSS feed submissions to services like Spotify.

Submit to Podcast Apps

Libsyn and Blubrry are both popular podcast hosting company options for podcasters. Libsyn is the biggest hosting company in the world, and it's generally regarded as the most functional and dependable. By using it, you can establish a presence on podcast apps.

Apple Podcasts has the biggest user base of all the podcast apps in the world, so it makes sense to start there. To do so, you will need to get Apple iTunes and Podcasts Connect accounts. Once you have an address for your RSS feed, you can log in to Podcasts Connect with your Apple iTunes login and select the option to add a Podcast. Then simply enter your RSS feed address. It will take several days for Apple to approve your show. When they do, they will send an email to the address associated with your iTunes account. Then you can begin releasing episodes.

Key Takeaways

In summary, when it comes to hosting your podcast, you should:

- Convert your show files from wav to mp3 or m4a file types
- Create an RSS feed
- Host your RSS feed on Lisbyn or Blubrry or a WordPress site (advanced)
- Sign up to Apple iTunes and Podcasts Connect to enter the RSS feed

13

FREE LAUNCH TACTICS

Creating a successful show requires you, as the host, to keep a number of considerations in your head and act in a manner that optimizes all of them. For a start, you have to host episodes, keep a steady release schedule, book guests if you have them, research podcast topics, oversee or implement editing, production and quality processes, and carry out a marketing strategy.

This might sound overwhelming, but it can all be broken into chunks. It's inadvisable to pay for advertising in the early stages, until you're up and running. The following launch tactics, should gain you early organic traffic with minimum spend.

Prepare to Launch

Just as many readers don't remember an author's name until they've read a number of their books, the same goes for podcast listeners and hosts. Launching a podcast with one episode won't make you a fixed part of a listener's life. It's a good idea to start with a handful of episodes already completed and uploaded before you launch.

Doing this work in advance will help you to develop a production system without the pressure of an upcoming deadline sitting on your shoulder.

Pitch as a Host and a Guest

Getting good guests is important for guest-based podcasts. Not only does their input determine the quality of your content, but their social clout can attract much-appreciated listeners. If you're not already a brand name in your industry, getting high-quality guests onto a new podcast can be a challenge. The key to having a high success rate is a good email pitch. Keep it relevant and focus on what you can do for them rather than what they can do for you. You wouldn't, for instance, ask Elon Musk to be featured on your poetry podcast because you're "a big fan" and he could "attract a lot of listeners." Instead, you might ask Rupi Kaur, because she is relevant, stating reasons why her work is interesting, and suggesting that she could gain some new fans because your podcast introduces new poetry enthusiasts to popular works in her genre.

You might want to start with lower-profile guests until you build a name for yourself. If you struggle to get early visitors, there's nothing wrong with running a few solo shows or even swapping appearances with other niche podcasters who understand your struggles. Pitch to other podcasters to be a guest on their show, outlining your area of expertise and suggesting why their listeners might be interested in you. Remember to be relevant, and aim to add value where possible as a guest and a host. This will attract more listeners to your show in the future.

Prepare Your Guests

Once you've bagged your first guest, it helps to prepare them in advance to make their experience as smooth as possible. Create a template email that briefs them on your show and outlines when and where it will be broadcast so that they can help promote it when their episode airs.

You could also add some promo graphics that they can share and a list of any technical requirements they will need to meet to ensure the recording goes without a hitch. Some podcasters even hand out instructions on the best ways to ensure a high-quality and well-lit video if they couple their audio podcast with a video feed.

Many guests also like to know what they are expected to talk about in advance. So, you could ask them for topic suggestions or, if you're highly organized, send them a list of questions you plan to ask based on their books. Building a good reputation as a host who runs a smooth operation can work in your favor over the long term.

Get Publicity

Also use your guests to help you promote your podcast. make it easy for our guests to share and promote their podcast episode. Send them a note on the day their podcast goes live and include a series of shareable media: e.g. pullquotes, images, links, prewritten tweets and status updates.

Social media and podcasting go really well together. Tease the next episode 24 hours ahead of time. Reshare each podcast episode multiple times. We do 3x to Twitter the first day, 2x to Facebook the first week. You could talk about the behind-the-scenes stuff in an Instagram story, post audiograms and quotes.

Aside from social media, there are several other ways you can publicise your podcast. Act as your own publicist by reaching out to journalists and other podcasters with ideas for news stories based around your show. It's not enough just to tell them that your show exists, that's not news. Journalists need a story. So you need an angle. Is your show about making money in some obscure discipline? "How This Author Makes Six Figures Selling Books for Cats" is a compelling headline journalists would be interested in investigating.

If you already have a mailing list for your books, then you could get some of your readers to champion your podcast and spread the word for your new show.

iTunes is responsible for as much as 70% of a podcast's listens and downloads so a lot of podcasters concentrate their promotional efforts there. The New & Noteworthy section of iTunes is one of the most highly visible spots in the iTunes podcast arena. You have two months (eight weeks) to get there before your podcast joins back with the rest of the podcast listings. Though they don't release the specifics of how podcasts are chosen for New & Noteworthy, iTunes seems to weigh the following factors quite heavily: number of subscriptions, downloads, and reviews in the eight weeks after launch.

But the main thing is content. If you have a good podcast, and you keep publishing new content consistently, listeners will find you.

Key Takeaways

In summary, when launching a show, you should:

- Practice your process by preparing a few episodes before launching episode one
- Craft a well-written pitch for prospective guests
- Pitch to be a guest on other people's podcasts
- Forge a reputation for being prepared and organized with guests
- Use publicity to gain an initial audience
- Focus on Apple iTunes New & Noteworthy

Long-Term Marketing Tactics

Podcasting is less competitive than blogging or vlogging but, given the rise of audio consumption, competition is growing. As a result, using free promotion methods and relying on organic traffic to grow your podcast will only get you so far. At some point, you need to look at more sure-fire ways to reach listeners.

As with books, the best marketing for a podcast is word-of-mouth, but people still need to find your content first to talk about it. Marketing your podcast requires learning a whole new skillset and can be its own challenge, but it is possible. In this chapter, we will explore a few strategies you can use to market your show and reach a wider audience.

Create a Strong Brand

The dictionary definition of branding is, "the promotion of a particular product or company by means of advertising and distinctive design." You might not consider your podcast a product or yourself a company, but you are and, as such, everything you do contributes to your brand, from the artwork you use to the guests you invite on your show.

Having a strong brand that is consistent across media platforms is vital if you want to generate brand recognition. Therefore, it's wise to use the same color palette, fonts, slogans, and image types on every promotional asset you produce, the first of which should be your logo.

Different podcast apps may list their own logo specifications, but that's okay. They will never be totally different so, once you've created one, you can usually just resize it to fit any criteria. For Apple Podcasts, for instance, the image must be:

- Between 1400x1400px & 3000x3000px
- Square
- Under 500kb in file size
- Saved with an RGB colorspace
- A jpg, jpeg, or a png file

If you have basic design skills, you can create a 1400x1400 logo on Photoshop or Canva. If you don't have these skills, you can commission a logo and then use a service like TinyPNG to shrink it to fit in the right file size. The logo should ideally look good both at full size and as a small thumbnail. Do this and it will attract more listeners on phone screens, but will also have more branding applications. Think of your book cover designs, and apply the same principles here, too.

Don't use images that you have found via Google Image Search or one on your computer that you didn't create. Doing so often breaches the copyright of the original creator. It's unethical and illegal unless you've paid for an image's license or have written permission to use it. You can license images legally at sites like Shutterstock.

Another thing to consider is the opening and closing music for your podcast. Like your logo artwork, your music will tie into your brand identity so should be constructed with care. Does an aggressive rap track really match a podcast about romantic poetry? Will it appeal to the right demographic? Perhaps, but the point is that you want to make this a conscious choice.

Don't pick a song just because you like it, and please don't illegally use copyrighted music. Make sure that you either find royalty-free music—for example from the iTunes Audio Library—or pay a musician and voice artist to create an entirely original soundtrack for you if you want something unique. A company like Music Radio Creative can provide this sort of service. There are also plenty of people on Fiverr who can achieve a similar result. Just ensure that, by doing this, you also obtain the necessary rights to use this soundtrack however you want as your brand grows.

Creating a strong brand, where all of the elements work together and appeal to the right audience, can help turn casual listeners into fans. Not only that, when combined, the factors lead listeners to associate your branded elements with you. Have you ever seen the Disney font on a poster and thought about Disney? Has a certain color of purple paint ever triggered you to think about Cadbury and crave chocolate? Good branding will create a similar sensation for your podcast.

Distribute Everywhere

Aggregators are distributor hubs that feed content onto different platforms. If you are a wide indie author (one who publishes books on lots of retailers), then you'll probably recognize e-book aggregators like Draft2Digital, Smashwords, and PublishDrive. Podcast aggregators work in a similar way; you share your files with one site, and they distribute to smaller ones on your behalf.

It's important that you make your podcast available to as many aggregators as possible to get maximum exposure. The biggest one is Apple Podcasts, but don't forget about Google Play, Spotify, iHeartRadio, Overcast, Stitcher, Soundcloud, and others. You'll need to create and submit an RSS feed for each of these services. It doesn't take up too much time, and it's worth it for discoverability.

This isn't necessarily a marketing tactic *per se*, but it does aid your promotional efforts because it makes your show easier to discover and access when someone hears about it. Plus, it makes your paid ads more likely to convert because it enables you to include more links and, thus, be relevant to a higher percentage of ad recipients.

Promote Your Back Catalog

Marketing becomes easier when you have more podcast episodes. There are two reasons for this:

- A larger range of content means that prospective listeners are more likely to find an episode that piques their interest.
- A backlist proves that you are a reliable content creator that newcomers can trust not to stop producing content once they are invested.

Producing and maintaining interest for lots of episodes can be one of your strongest marketing strategies. So, don't focus entirely on launching new content at the expense of fully exploiting your back catalogue. You never know what opportunities you can seize by using the IP you've already created. This is especially true if something comes up in the news that makes it even more relevant. Try to make your podcasts as "evergreen" as possible so you can continue to promote them long after they air.

Drive SEO

Search Engine Optimization (SEO) is changing due to a rise in voice-assisted devices in people's homes. As a result, more users than ever are bypassing typing and opting to search with their voices. This means that keyword phrases attached to your metadata need to read more naturally because the average users speak differently than the way they type.

Still, if you want to make your podcast more searchable, then creating good metadata is essential. Leaving snippets and concise meta descriptions of your podcast is paramount as is writing keyword-rich episode titles. Transcripts can also help improve discoverability. What is your podcast about in a nutshell? What search terms are listeners most likely to use to find it? Paid advertising can create a surge in listens, but only good metadata can draw in an organic audience. In an increasingly crowded field, choosing the right keywords can mean the difference between attracting a huge audience and not getting one at all.

Prioritize Your Website

Your website is your home base and is where you should drive as many listeners as you can. There are many reasons for this as a marketer, including the following:

- Visitors get added value because of the links, resources, and show notes that you can't include on podcast apps.
- A webpage you've created is easier to share than an app page, especially if you've designed it to include an appropriate social sharing plug-in.
- It enables you to control the viewing experience and advertise your mailing list sign-up, which you can use to market to visitors again for free in the future.

Use Paid Advertising

Paid advertising comes in many forms. Historically, it was simple. You could pay a one-off fee and have your ad circulated in a magazine or emblazoned onto a billboard. That's still possible, but many web-based companies prefer digital advertising solutions because of their targeting options and scalability. For podcasts, you can advertise to podcast listeners directly on podcast apps. Spotify and Overcast both provide paid advertising options as do many of their competitors. Their targeting options, however, are fairly broad.

For a more nuanced approach, you should run Facebook ads directly to your podcast on your website. This strategy can become expensive if you don't know what you're doing. Plus, you can't guarantee that the people receiving your ads are podcast listeners like you can with the in-app options. But if you test them and drill down to the correct audience, they can deliver stellar results.

Just remember that paid ads aren't the key to guaranteed long-term success. Over time, you would be better off producing an excellent show that listeners recommend and building a mailing list to promote new episodes to your existing audience. In the meantime, ads can help you get to that position.

Upscale Your Guests

It can be difficult to attract powerful guests to your podcast when you start recording, but it gets easier as your listenership grows. With more listeners come higher-profile guests, which initiates a virtual cycle. You can even mention prominent previous guests in your own pitches to attract even bigger names, and then ask those newcomers to help promote your show.

If any of your guests have a large audience, make it easy for them to share a link with their followers on social media. Having ready-made pull-quotes with links is one way to make the guest's job as easy as possible and maximize the help you receive. Sending them extra information, along with graphics, reduces the workload involved in sharing your podcast and their potential resistance.

Ask Your Audience

Creators in general have a hard time asking their audiences for help, but many listeners and even readers who don't listen to your podcast but love your books will spread the word if you ask them. Make it easy for them to access your podcast by sharing links and audio snippets on social media. In doing so, tailor your message to pique the curiosity of followers who are interested in your niche topic for best results.

Twitter already makes it easy to share sound snippets, or even entire podcasts, with Libsyn, Soundcloud, and other audio hosting services. YouTube videos are also easy to share on most platforms. Just remember to include a strong call to action alongside your content to make your followers are more likely to share and retweet.

Being an active member of a relevant online community can also be a huge benefit. By sharing your episodes with your community, you'll offer content directly to your target audience, which can drive downloads substantially if you put in the groundwork to add value before asking for help.

Posting on social media can be time consuming, but it doesn't have to be if you systematize your work. To automate the process of posting across several platforms, check out tools like Zapier and Hootsuite. Both online social media schedulers help users to prepare and schedule posts in advance, so they don't have to spend hours every day to offer a consistent presence. By using schedulers, you can distribute a variety of posts at different times on auto-pilot, both for creating engagement and spreading your message.

Repurpose Your Content

Your presence on multiple social media platforms will broaden your reach and expand your network potential, but only if you remember to adapt your style to look native on each individual platform. This is called repurposing your content. That might mean using the same graphic and message but including hashtags on Twitter and switching up the text-to-image ratio for Facebook or Instagram. Or it could mean scheduling tweets once every hour compared to publishing a twice weekly Facebook post. There's a lot consider, but the right repurposing process can turn your social media strategy into a slick, powerful procedure.

For example, to maximize your reach and attract more listeners, you could:

- Record your podcast as a long-form video for YouTube
- Cut the video into soundbites for TikTok and a second YouTube channel
- Tease out the long-form audio for podcast apps
- Convert video stills into thumbnail images and apply quotes for Instagram and Twitter

- Edit a short video of highlights that includes cliffhangers, and apply links for social media
- Get a transcript and repurpose it as a blog post or book chapter

Each of these individual content streams won't necessarily have a noticeable impact, but their collective power, when delivered consistently over time, can make you a constant presence in the eyes of your fans. Plus, they weatherproof you from changes in the industry. If one set of fans disappears, you can rely on another platform to pick up the slack.

Ask for Reviews

Getting time-starved listeners to take a chance on your podcast can prove difficult without having any social proof to persuade them it's a good idea. Getting a few positive reviews and ratings on the major podcast apps can improve your click-through rates and lead to more long-term fans. The problem that many new podcasters face is getting those early reviews.

Asking your online communities, and even friends and family, to help support you by subscribing to your podcast and leaving you a rating and review is a good way to begin. Subscriptions, ratings, and reviews are three components that many podcast apps use to determine your ranking amongst other podcasts, so this early assistance can really help, particularly if that initial influx is substantial enough to get your show onto a chart for your niche.

Drumming up long-term support is challenging unless you have a plan. That's where a review-generating campaign comes into play. There are a few tactics you can deploy to begin building reviews over time to keep scaling your show. One is to ask listeners for reviews during your podcast. This might make you uncomfortable at first, but listeners won't mind if you regularly ask for ratings and reviews on your podcast. They also won't mind if you incorporate a call-to-action (CTA) in your social media.

According to Hootsuite, CTAs drastically improve the chances of your getting someone to take action. They prompt them with the idea and channel their focus into doing the one thing that you want them to do. Just remember to keep it simple. People will often do what you ask if it's only one thing, but giving five different CTAs may result in no action at all. Don't ask listeners to subscribe to your podcast, sign up to your newsletter, rate, review, and share. Pick whichever is most important, and stick to it.

Work to Your Strengths

Forming a marketing strategy is an individual experience because everyone's audience acts differently and not every tactic will work for your podcast. As a result, the only way to find out what works for you is to experiment. Test paid ads, try multiple distribution channels, invite a variety of guests, and figure out different ways to ask for reviews. Eventually, you will find a handful of methods that make a difference and that you enjoy.

Key Takeaways

In summary, when marketing your podcast, you should:

- Come up with graphics, text, and audio content that form a cohesive brand
- Distribute widely to make your podcast as accessible as possible
- Create more content because nothing promotes your last episode like your next one
- Optimize your metadata to be SEO-friendly
- Prioritize your website to maximize your control over your exposure
- Test paid advertising options until you find one with a good return on investment
- Approach more prominent guests as your reputation grows, but keep them relevant
- Repurpose your content to attract listeners from different places
- Develop a strategy that achieves your goals and is also one that you enjoy

❀ Created with Vellum

14

KEEP GOING

Various sources on the internet claim that most podcasts stop after six episodes. Whether this is true is unclear, but what's certain is that many fail, not because something causes them to stop, but because their hosts stop trying. Realistically, launching a podcast is a lot of work, even if you're only doing it as a hobby and don't plan to make money. Hosts have to wear several hats, juggle a number of techy and creative tasks, and coordinate their efforts with guests. Being a guest only entails a fraction of the workload, but it does still require some effort.

All of this toil sometimes seems pointless when you don't see immediate returns, but it pays to keep going. Just like books, podcasts take time to gain traction. Early results are small, and the rewards are infrequent, but over time the results build exponentially. Yes, some people see success faster and fly higher while others make slow progress and never reach the stratosphere, but almost everyone who perseveres sees some sort of progress. As such, the final piece of advice in this guide is to keep going. With practice, running your podcast will get easier, your episodes will get better, and you rewards will get bigger. You just have to fight through the doubt and keep moving until the tide turns in your favor.

15

GLOSSARY

The definitions offered here represent the meanings understood and shared by the majority of the global podcasting community and the Alliance of Independent Authors.

The glossary includes both technical and business terms and uses US spellings. Additionally, it covers the most popular brand names used by industry experts, as they too can confuse. Each podcasting service and company has its own specialized jargon that authors need to understand in order to communicate effectively with the services they use.

Brand names are capitalized to distinguish them from the other terms.

Terms that have more than a single meaning have numbered definitions, beginning with the most common and proceeding to the more obscure. As a guiding principle, when in doubt, we've opted for over-defining as safer than under-defining.

The intent throughout is to define and explain terms in plain language as much as possible. Some definitions are tentative since podcasting is a new field. Definitions will evolve in this field as will the creative business knowledge and expertise of the creators who inhabit it.

Adobe Audition

Video and audio editing software produced by Adobe.

Amazon S3

Amazon Simple Storage Service (S3) provides an internet storage solution. It has a simple web services interface that you can use to store and retrieve any amount of data, at any time, from anywhere on the web.

Answer the Public

A search listening tool users can harness to produce search insights and keyword recommendations.

Apple CarPlay

An Apple standard app that enables a car radio or head unit to be a display and a controller for an iOS device. Users commonly use it to listen to iTunes or Apple Podcasts in their car.

Apple iTunes

An entertainment app created by Apple that allows users to store, curate, and play audio content.

Apple Podcasts

A podcast-playing app produced by Apple that is regarded as one of the most popular in the world.

Apple Podcasts Connect

A program run by Apple that enables independent podcast creators to publish their podcasts within the Apple content ecosystem.

Audacity

A multi-track audio editor and recorder for Windows, macOS, Linux, and other operating systems.

bandwidth

The data capacity of a computer network in bits per second (Bps).

Blubrry

A podcast hosting and distribution company used by independent creators and corporate networks.

Bluetooth

A short-range wireless technology standard used for exchanging data between fixed and mobile devices over short distances.

Cleanfeed

A browser-based collaboration tool for live audio and recording.

ECamm Call Recorder

A piece of software you can use in combination with Skype to record video sessions, podcasts, and interviews as you see them or in a side-by-side and split-screen mode.

Google Search

A search engine created by Google that handles billions of searches per day.

Google Trends

A web-based Google tool anyone can use for free to compare the relative popularity of different search terms.

hosting

The function of a web server that stores and transmits data for one or more websites.

iTunes

see: **Apple iTunes**

JPEG

A format for compressing image files; the most common image format used by digital cameras.

JPG

see: **JPEG**

Libsyn

A service that offers podcast hosting and analytics options for podcasters.

M4A

A file extension for an audio file. It was originally intended to replace the MP3 file type, which had not been designed for audio.

MP3

An audio file format commonly used for music, audiobooks, and podcast files.

Music Radio Creative

An online service that provides paid and royalty-free solutions for music, voiceovers, and jingles which can be used by podcasters, DJs, and traditional radio networks.

Overcast

A podcast aggregator that parses your RSS feed and distributes your podcast to listeners.

Pamela

Free audio and video recording software that is compatible with Skype.

PlayerFM

A podcast aggregator app available for Apple and Android mobile devices.

plug-in

A software component that adds a specific feature to an existing computer program. Plug-ins can be client based or browser based. When a program supports plug-ins, it enables customization.

PNG

PNG stands for "Portable Graphics Format." It is the most commonly used uncompressed raster image file format on the internet. The best way to identify a PNG format is to see it if has a clear background layer rather than the white background layer that characterizes the JPEG file type.

Pocket Casts

A podcast-playing app owned by four major US radio networks. It is open to content from radio stations and independent podcast creators.

Quicktime

A Mac-only software option that podcasters can use to record their side of a conversation locally while their guest records their side locally on their device.

RSS feed

A record-like file type that collects news and web content from one or more internet-based outlets so that it can be fed to various websites.

Skype

Free software developed by Microsoft that facilitates video and audio calls between users as well as messaging capabilities.

Skype Credits

Purchasable tokens a Skype user can cash in to make a Skype call to a phone line or send messages via SMS.

Soundcloud

An online audio distribution platform and music-sharing website founded in Sweden but based in Germany. It enables its users to upload, promote, and share audio content. It also enables listeners to stream audio.

Spotify

A prominent audio-streaming app that includes a massive catalogue of music and podcasts, all of which is served to listeners via a sophisticated recommendation algorithm.

Stitcher

A popular podcast listening app available to Apple and Android users.

streaming

A method of transmitting or receiving audio and video files over a computer network as a continuous flow. This process allows for live content viewing as well as playback while the rest of the content streams.

TinyPNG

A service that uses smart lossy compression techniques to reduce the size of your PNG files.

USB port

A standard cable connection port on computers and consumer electronics that allows for short-distance digital data communications.

WAV

A file format used for storing uncompressed audio files.

WordPress

The world's most popular website-building platform.

Zoom

A video conferencing tool used for one-on-one conversations as well as live webinars pumped out to thousands of guests.

THE END

ACKNOWLEDGMENTS

All good books are a team effort. An author's name goes on the cover but behind that is the creative team of editors and designers and formatters who made the book, the distributors and marketers who take it to readers, and the long list of supporters—from family members to work colleagues—without whom it would never have been created.

Then there are the other writers, from journalists and academics to storytellers and poets, who have published relevant ideas, information and inspirations that, quite literally, underwrite the book.

All this is true for this book you hold in your hand and our thanks to all those who had a hand in its making.

Thanks are due to all at the Alliance of Independent Authors (ALLi). ALLi guides rely heavily on the work and wisdom of our team, members, ambassadors and advisors. All of this is generously and freely shared with our non-profit CIC (Community Interest Company), with the intention of paying it forward, and benefitting other indie authors. Thank you for your generosity and for lighting the way.

For this guide to podcasting for authors, particular thanks to the creative team members Tim Lewis, Howard Lovy, Dan Parsons, Orna Ross and Lauren Johnson.

And to all the ALLi members and advisors who have contributed experiences and given us permission to quote their work and their ideas in this book: thank you for your generosity and for lighting the way.

And, thank you, self-publishing indie author, for reading (and reviewing) this book.

16
ABOUT ALLI

ALLi, the Alliance of Independent Authors is the global association for self-publishing indie authors.

Join us for reliable advice and advocacy,
discounts, free guidebooks and resources, member forums, contract review, motivation, education and support from a wonderful indie author community.
AllianceIndependentAuthors.org

More Advice & Feedback

17

MORE ADVICE

We'd love to send you a weekly roundup
of self-publishing advice
from our award-winning blog.

Sign up here for the best tips and tools from the Alliance of
Independent Authors
Delivered to your inbox each Wednesday

18

WE'D LOVE YOUR FEEDBACK

Review Request

If you enjoyed this book, would you consider leaving a brief review online on your favorite online bookstore that takes reviews: Amazon, Apple, Barnes and Noble, Goodreads or Kobo?

A good review is very important to authors these days as it helps other readers know this is a book worth their time.

It doesn't have to be long or detailed. Just a sentence saying what you enjoyed and a star-rating is all that's needed. Many thanks.

Podcasting for Authors

copyright © Alliance Independent Authors 2021

ebook: 978-1-913588-69-4
Paperback: 978-1-913588-70-0
Large Print: 978-1-913588-71-7
Hardback: 978-1-913588-72-4
Audio: 978-1-913588-73-1

The authors's moral rights have been asserted. All rights reserved.

Enquiries: info@ornaross.com